THE WORLD HERITAGE

ANCIENT GREECE

CHILDRENS PRESS®
CHICAGO

Table of Contents

Library of Congress Cataloging-in-Publication Data

Terzi, Marinella.
  [Antigua Grecia. English]
  Ancient Greece / by Marinella Terzi.
    p. cm. — (The World heritage)
  Translation of: La antigua Grecia.
  Includes index.
  Summary: Discusses the culture of ancient Greece and examines the temples, statues, and other physical remains of that time.
  ISBN 0-516-08376-7
  1. Greece—Civilization—To 146 B.C.—Juvenile literature. [1. Greece—Civilization—To 146 B.C. 2. Greece—Antiquities.] I. Title. II. Series.
DF77.T4713 1992
938—dc20
                                    92-7508
                                    CIP
                                    AC

La Antigua Grecia: © INCAFO S.A./Ediciones S.M./UNESCO 1990
Ancient Greece: © Childrens Press, Inc./UNESCO 1992

ISBN (UNESCO) 92-3-102596-1
ISBN (Childrens Press) 0-516-08376-7

Ancient Greece

If Greece had never existed, our lives today would be very different. Many aspects of the world we live in come directly from ancient Greece. Democratic government, sports competitions, the design of buildings, ways of thinking and arguing, ideas in literature and theater, ideas about beauty . . . all of these are part of the heritage left to us by the Greeks.

Greece today is a small, mountainous country on the Balkan Peninsula. It extends down from eastern Europe into the Mediterranean Sea. West of Greece, across the Ionian Sea, is Italy. To the east is the Aegean Sea and Asia Minor, where Turkey is today. The southern part of Greece, actually a large peninsula, is known as Peloponnesus or the Peloponnese. Dozens of islands are scattered in the surrounding waters of the Aegean and Mediterranean seas.

Greek culture once flourished on the islands and shores all around present-day Greece. Art, music, drama, and literature thrived. Poetry and plays, temples and theaters, sculpture and pottery—all reached for the highest ideals of beauty and perfection. Today we can admire the Greeks' ideals in the writings, artworks, and monuments they left behind.

Descendants of the Greeks
Today's world is directly descended from the Greeks' world. They gave us patterns that we still follow. They were masters in the art of government, the fathers of philosophy, and great writers and sculptors. Many of their works live on, centuries later, such as these details from the Acropolis. (*Left*) A group of sculptures preserved in the Acropolis Museum. (*Right*) The pedestal of the Quadriga of Agrippa.

Centuries of History

There were people living in Greece more than 8,000 years ago. We know this from the work of archaeologists—scientists who study remains from the past. The oldest villages they have found belong to a period known as the Paleolithic, or Old Stone Age. Ancient Greece's Neolithic, or New Stone Age, began after about 6000 B.C. That's when farming villages first appeared. These early farmers grew wheat and barley and kept domesticated, or tamed, animals such as dogs and sheep.

Greece's **Early Period**, or Bronze Age, lasted from about 3000 B.C. to 1150 B.C. The brilliant Minoan culture flourished on the island of Crete (see map on page 15). Minoan traders sailed to Egypt and other lands bordering the Mediterranean Sea.

The Mycenaeans appeared on the Greek mainland about 1600 B.C. They adopted much of Minoan culture, conquered Crete, and set up colonies throughout the Mediterranean world. Fierce Mycenaean warriors raided coastal towns. In about 1250 B.C., they attacked the city of Troy. We know of the Trojan War from the *Iliad*, an epic poem by the Greek poet Homer.

The **Middle Period** of Greek history lasted from 1150 B.C. to 800 B.C. Culture and trade declined, and so did settlements in new territories. This is sometimes called Greece's "Dark Age." At this time, the Greek people organized themselves into city-states. Each city-state, or *polis*, was made up of a large city and its surrounding land. City-states were separate units that governed themselves. But they all shared the same customs, language, and religion.

The **Greek Renaissance** period (800 B.C. to 480 B.C.) was a time of new ideas and great projects. Greeks began to use metal coins and an alphabet. They started new colonies around the Mediterranean shores and traded far and wide. Philosophers looked for new ways to explain the world of nature, and poets wrote epic and lyric poems. Sculptors, potters, and painters created brilliant works of art. In 508 B.C., the city-state of Athens became a democracy—a government by vote of the citizens.

Greece's **Classical Period** lasted from 480 B.C. to 338 B.C. Invaders from the Persian Empire tried to conquer the Greeks in 490 and 480 B.C., but the Greeks fought them off. After the Persian Wars, Athens united the islands and cities around the Aegean Sea. This union was called the Delian League, but it was really an Athenian Empire.

Dwellings of the Gods
The Greek temples were built on sacred ground as dwellings for the gods. Two examples are shown in the photos on the opposite page. (*Top*) The temple of Delphi, consecrated to the god Apollo. (*Below*) The Erechtheum, honoring Athena, Poseidon, and the king Erechtheus, in the Acropolis at Athens.

Olympic Games: In Honor of Zeus

Zeus, according to Greek mythology, hurled a bolt of lightning to indicate the place where he was to be honored. An altar and a pyre were built there, and offerings to the gods were burned on them. A race was run to decide which youth would have the honor of lighting the pyre. That is the story of how the Olympic Games began.

The first sports festival was held at Olympia in 776 B.C. From that time on, the Olympic Games took place every four years for the next 1,170 years! Then the Roman emperor Theodosius had them stopped.

The first modern Olympic Games took place in Athens in 1896. Their promoter was a Frenchman, Pierre de Fredy, Baron of Coubertin. Marble from the quarries of Mt. Pendeli was used in constructing the new stadium. Stone from the same quarries had been used, many centuries earlier, for building the Parthenon.

The Symbol of Greek Art

The Acropolis is the outstanding symbol of Greek art. It is located on a rocky promontory 500 feet (150 meters) high, covering an area of about 7.5 acres (3 hectares). The fortress has passed through many stages through the years. There was already an acropolis (a "high city") in the same place over a thousand years before Christ. Some remnants of its protective wall, known as the Pelasgian Wall, are still there. The photo shows the Acropolis as seen from Mt. Philopappus. Crowning the promontory is the Parthenon, in Doric style, built in honor of the goddess Athena. At the foot of the Acropolis is the Odeum, or music hall, of Herodes Atticus.

The period from 462 to 429 B.C. is called the Age of Pericles, in honor of a great statesman of Athens.

From 431 to 404 B.C., Athens and Sparta fought each other in the Peloponnesian War. While war was raging, many Athenians—including Pericles himself—died of a plague. Athens was weakened by political confusion and the strain of war, and the Spartans won. But Athens rebelled and set up its democracy again after only a year of Spartan rule.

In the **Hellenistic Age** (338 B.C. to 196 B.C.), Philip of Macedonia unified Greece. His son, Alexander the Great, ruled from 336 to 323 B.C. Alexander conquered the Persian Empire and spread Greek culture from Egypt to India. He had a great idea of the unity of all peoples. After he died, the Greek world broke up into several smaller kingdoms. Piece by piece, the Romans gradually conquered the Greek-speaking lands.

Daily Life and Customs

Social life in ancient Greece centered around the agora, or public square and marketplace. Public buildings, temples, and law courts stood in the agora. There, too, politicians and philosophers would meet and express their ideas freely.

In contrast to the beautiful temples were the humble mud-brick cottages of the common people. There was no sewage system, and garbage was thrown on the streets. Foul smells rose from dirty alleyways.

Theater Lovers
The Greeks loved drama so much that they built many theaters. Several plays would take place one after another. The chorus, made up only of men, was important to the narrative of the plays. The members of the chorus wore masks and cothurni, or high laced boots. Examples of Greek theaters are the Odeum of Herodes Atticus in Athens (*top right*), built in Roman times, and the theater at Delphi (*bottom right*).

In the photo at the left are Doric columns of the temple of Apollo the Healer in Bassae.

Residence of the Pythia

At first, the oracle of Delphi was consulted once a year. But as the number of appeals increased, the oracle was called on once a month. The Pythia, a woman through whose mouth the god Apollo spoke, gave answers to requests for advice. The ritual was quite complicated. Petitioners were purified at the Castalian Spring. Then they sacrificed an animal, and the Pythia performed certain rituals.

One structure at the archaeological site of Delphi is the sanctuary of Athena Pronaos. All that is left of this building today, as shown in the photo, are three columns topped with a section of the frieze and cornice.

Much of the population were slaves. Those who worked in private homes had an easier time than others. They were well fed, and some had a chance to earn their freedom. On the other hand, slaves who worked in mines and quarries led a truly hard life.

But it was the common people and the slaves who baked the beautiful pottery, rowed great ships, cast bronze and iron, and raised almost all the food. Stone by stone, they built Greece's architectural monuments, many of which are still standing today.

Women did not have many rights. They could not take part in Greek politics, social life, or arts. (One exception was the great female poet Sappho.) A woman's father or husband was considered her guardian. Upper-class women could not go out on the street alone.

Athens was a democracy during the Classical Period. Common citizens then had a voice in their government. Only free Greek men were counted as citizens, though. Women, slaves, and foreigners could not vote.

Young men received a serious education. They learned reading and writing, music and singing, and the reciting of poetry. Physical training was very important. For the Greeks, the body of a young man represented beauty and perfection. A youth had to exercise hard to attain even greater beauty.

Timeline of Ancient Greek History

(All dates are approximate.)

3000-1150 B.C.	Bronze Age; people settle in Greek mainland and nearby islands
2900-1200 B.C.	Minoan culture flourishes on Crete
1600-1150 B.C.	Mycenaeans inhabit Greek mainland and expand throughout the Mediterranean
1250 B.C.	Trojan War
800-480 B.C.	Greek Renaissance period; Greeks found colonies throughout the Mediterranean; philosophy, poetry, and the arts flourish
776 B.C.	First sports festival at Olympia
508 B.C.	Athens becomes a democracy
500-479 B.C.	Persian Wars
462-429 B.C.	Age of Pericles; height of Athenian democracy; construction of the Acropolis
431-404 B.C.	Peloponnesian War between Athens and Sparta
338 B.C.	Philip of Macedonia unites all of Greece
336-323 B.C.	Rule of Alexander the Great
323 B.C.	Death of Alexander; division of Greek lands
200 B.C.	Roman Empire begins gradual domination of Greece

The Greek Domains
Like all people who lived by the sea, the Greeks were travelers and merchants. Through the centuries, they spread out over the Aegean and Ionian Seas. The cities on the coasts of Asia Minor, southern Italy, and the island of Sicily became part of the Greek world (right).

A Refined Culture
Words were very important to the Greeks, and they took the time to listen. They were fond of oratory, poetry recitations, and plays. Performances always took place in open-air theaters, with rising rows of seats. This photo shows the theater of Dionysus below the Acropolis.

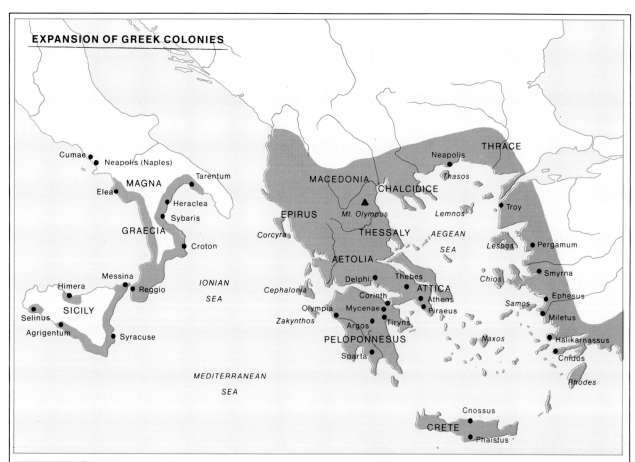

EXPANSION OF GREEK COLONIES

Cumae
Neapolis (Naples)
MAGNA
Tarentum
Elea
Heraclea
GRAECIA
Sybaris
Croton
Messina
Himera
Reggio
SICILY
Selinus
Agrigentum
Syracuse

IONIAN
SEA

THRACE
Neapolis
MACEDONIA
Thasos
CHALCIDICE
EPIRUS
Mt. Olympus
Troy
Lemnos
THESSALY
AEGEAN
Corcyra
SEA
Lesbos
Pergamum
AETOLIA
Chios
Smyrna
Delphi
Thebes
Cephalonia
Corinth
ATTICA
Ephesus
Olympia
Mycenae
Athens
Samos
Miletus
Zakynthos
Piraeus
Argos
Tiryns
Halikarnassus
PELOPONNESUS
Naxos
Cnidus
Sparta
Rhodes

MEDITERRANEAN
SEA

Cnossus
CRETE
Phaistus

There were many types of athletic training. One was a contest in five events, similar to the present-day pentathlon. It included wrestling, running, javelin throw, long jump, and discus throw.

Beginning in 776 B.C., athletic games for all of Greece were held at Olympia. The Olympic Games took place every four years from then until A.D. 393, when Roman conquerors put a stop to them. Cities and colonies competed fiercely against each other. Athletes struggled so hard to win that they sometimes damaged their health or even died of exhaustion.

During the games, political activity and battles came to a halt. Philosophers, politicians, and writers gave speeches to show off their talents at the games.

Women did not compete in the Olympics. However, there was a separate women's athletic event at Olympia called the festival of Hera.

The Greeks were fond of great feasts. These events could last for hours, with plenty of food, drink, and entertainment. The Greeks used these banquets to exchange ideas, since they enjoyed good conversation. Their wives did not come to these feasts, but the hetaeras did. Hetaeras were women who played the flute, danced, attended the men, and often joined in the conversation.

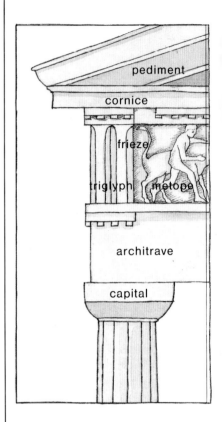

Gods and Temples

The earliest Greeks worshipped the Mother Goddess. A famous image of her still stands in Ephesus, Turkey. Little by little, more gods were taken on. They were said to live on Mt. Olympus.

There were twelve main gods, known as the Olympians:

Zeus was the supreme god, the god of the heavens. His wife, Hera, was the goddess of heaven. Athena was the goddess of war, the arts, and intelligence. Apollo was the god of the sun, poetry, and song. Artemis was the goddess of hunting and the woods. Hermes was the god of commerce, shepherds, and travelers on foot. Aphrodite was the goddess of fertility and love. Poseidon was god of the sea and navigation. Hestia was goddess of the home. (Dionysus, god of wine, is sometimes named in place of Hestia.) Demeter was goddess of the earth and agriculture. Ares was the god of war. And Hephaestus was the god of fire, the forge, and metalworking.

The Temples, Masterpieces of Architecture

Most of the architectural works still standing in Greece are temples. Houses were built of non-permanent materials such as unbaked mud-bricks. The temples, however, were built of stones or marble slabs that were simply placed on top of each other. The Greeks did not use mortar or cement as building materials. H-shaped bronze clamps, set in place with molten lead, were sometimes used to hold the stones together. Columns were important parts of these structures. (*Opposite page, top*) The Propylaea, the entrance to the Acropolis in Athens. (*Bottom*) The temple of Apollo the Healer at Bassae. Both belong to the classical period of Greek art.

The gods and goddesses were at the very heart of Greek life. Their presence was felt in everything the people did. The Greeks built temples to honor their various gods. In front of each temple was an altar, where sacrifices of animals or farm products were offered. This was a way to obtain the gods' protection against misfortune and sickness, and forgiveness for bad conduct.

Divination was another common practice. This was the art of predicting the future or discovering hidden truths. Divination could be done in a number of ways—for example, by reading meanings in the flight of birds or the insides of sacrificed animals. Other divinations came from the oracles, persons who were believed to speak for the gods. The oracle of Delphi was one of the most popular. Pilgrims traveled there from all over Greece and even from foreign lands.

The Greeks thought that the oracle always spoke the truth. If something didn't turn out the way the oracle had said, it was because people did not know how to interpret the words of the god correctly. Thus the oracle always kept its good reputation.

Arts and Sciences

Poetry was a fine art in ancient Greece. During festivals, male performers called rhapsodes recited poems. Dances or the music of a lyre or flute often accompanied their words. Before the alphabet was introduced, around 800 B.C., poems were passed along orally from father to son. That is why we have so few written poems from early times.

Epic poems were those that told stories about great heroes from the past. Greece's most famous epic poems are Homer's *Iliad* and *Odyssey*. The *Iliad* tells about the Trojan War. Its 15,000 verses are written in hexameter, or lines with six stressed syllables. The *Odyssey* is made up of 11,000 hexameter verses. It tells of the action-packed journey of Odysseus to his home after fighting in the Trojan War. The gods play a central role in both poems. Homer wrote these works in the eighth century B.C., but the events he describes took place 500 years earlier.

Drama was both a serious art and a popular entertainment. Lighthearted plays that ended happily were comedies, and those that ended with misfortune were tragedies. Satyr plays were comedies that made fun of the gods and their activities.

The Propylaea of the Acropolis
Visitors are astonished by the size and beauty of the columns at the entrance to the Acropolis. They are part of the Propylaea, built in 437 B.C. The entryway consists of six Doric columns grouped in two sets of three columns each. Two platforms rise to the sides, with three Ionic columns on each of them. These are considered by many to be the most perfect Ionic columns in the world.

Every spring, Greeks held an event called the Dionysian festival. Three tragedies (a "trilogy") were performed in one day, followed by a brief satyr play. This was done for three days in a row. On another day, three comedies were performed.

The chorus played an important role in Greek drama. It commented on events in the play and sometimes took part in the action. The chorus was composed entirely of men, who wore masks and high laced boots called cothurni. All the actors were men, too.

Many theaters were built throughout the Greek world. One of the finest is the theater at Epidaurus. Ordinary citizens were welcome to attend the theaters. If they were poor, the state paid their admission fee.

Another heritage from the Greek world is philosophy. In the sixth century B.C., some thinkers of Miletus, on the coast of Asia Minor, could not believe that the gods caused everything to happen. They tried to explain nature and the universe through reason. Thales, Anaximander, and Anaximenes were the main thinkers of this school. Other philosophers appeared in the fifth and fourth centuries B.C. The most famous were Socrates, his pupil Plato, and Aristotle.

Some Greeks had a special talent for physics and mechanics. Archimedes spent many years building elaborate war machines. Others built great reputations as doctors. The physician Hippocrates taught that a doctor should study a sick person's symptoms instead of consulting the gods. Today doctors make a pledge called the Hippocratic oath, promising to follow the highest standards of their profession.

DORIC   IONIC   CORINTHIAN

Art Immersed in Nature
The Greeks knew how to take advantage of their landscape. They always chose the most suitable place to build their temples and fortresses. The site of Delphi is certainly one of the most beautiful in the country. As for the Acropolis, the hill it stands on is visible from every part of Athens. (*Top*) The Agora and Sacred Way of the sanctuary of Apollo in Delphi. (*Below*) A view of the Athenian Acropolis.

Mathematics, astronomy, and geometry were the major sciences of the ancient Greeks. Their geometry skills are best shown in their architecture. Today, temples, theaters, stadiums, tombs, and other monuments remain as examples of the Greeks' architectural skills. Only a few remnants of houses remain, since they were made of materials such as mud-bricks.

There were three "orders," or styles, of Greek architecture: Doric, Ionic, and Corinthian. The difference is in the columns. Doric columns have no base, and their capitals, or top parts, are simple and severe. Ionic columns stand on a base. Their capitals are decorated with volutes, or scrolls. Corinthian columns are like Ionic columns, only with acanthus leaves decorating the capitals.

Sculpture was the finest of Greek arts. The earliest statues stand stiff and straight. Little by little, sculptors gave their statues a feeling of movement. Most sculptures were done in marble or bronze. Many Greek statues have no definite front. The head and the body face different ways, so they can be viewed from any angle.

The principal sculptors were Phidias, Myron, Praxiteles, and Lysippus.

The Greeks created wall paintings called murals and frescoes. But their best surviving paintings are found on vases and other pottery. Using brushes made from human hair, they painted with extremely fine lines.

Black-on-red pottery—with black figures against a red background—originated in Corinth. It quickly spread to Athens, where it became more popular than in Corinth. Around 500 B.C., Athenian artists began to create red-on-black pottery. Here, the drawing skills were even better than in the earlier black-on-red pottery.

Temple of Apollo the Healer at Bassae

In the fifth century B.C., the people of Phigalia prayed to Apollo to save them from the plague. They were spared, and in thanks they dedicated a temple to Apollo the Healer. The temple's ruins stand at an altitude of 3,700 feet (1,130 meters) in the Arcadian Mountains near Bassae, in the heart of the Peloponnese.

Historians believe that this temple may have been built by Ictinus. He was one of the main architects of the Parthenon, the grand temple of Athena in Athens. This would explain how a temple in such an out-of-the-way place could be so excellent.

Dedicated to the God of Healing
The temple at Bassae was dedicated to Apollo the Healer, who had come to the aid of the people during an outbreak of the plague. The temple may have been the work of Ictinus, chief architect of the Parthenon. This would explain how such a fine building could be found in a rather unimportant spot. The photos at the right show the exterior and interior of the temple at Bassae.

The outside of the temple is in the Doric style, and its interior is Ionic. It also has just one Corinthian column. The building is made of a yellowish-gray limestone with striking red-and-white streaks, abundant in the region. Marble is used for the most prominent parts, such as the Corinthian column.

Besides the lone Corinthian column, the temple has some other unusual features. It is lined up along a north-south axis. The columns on the northern side are much thicker than those on the southern face. Columns on the inside are attached to the walls. It is also rare at such an early date for Doric, Ionic, and Corinthian styles to be combined in one building.

The Archaeological Site at Epidaurus

In southeastern Greece, across the Saronic Gulf from Athens, lie the ruins of Epidaurus. In the fourth century B.C., Epidaurus was the center for worship of Asclepius, the god of medicine. At the site are the temple of Asclepius, a great theater, a gymnasium, baths, and a *tholos*, a round building for religious use.

Constant pilgrimages made their way to Epidaurus. Sick people were attracted to its gymnasium and baths. They were also encouraged to sleep on the portico of the temple of Asclepius. It was believed that, in their dreams, the god revealed the way they could be healed. Accounts of many miraculous cures are recorded in stone inscriptions at the site.

The Most Beautiful Theater in the World

Perfectly proportioned, with ideal acoustics, the theater of Epidaurus is one of the best preserved in Greece. It was designed in the fourth century B.C. by the architect Polyclitus the Younger, according to the geographer Pausanias. It could hold 14,000 people. Its fame spread when the Romans arrived in Greece. By the time of the emperor Hadrian, it was known as the most beautiful theater in the world. Still as useful a theater as ever, it has been the site of an annual festival of plays since 1955.

Terms in Greek Architecture

architrave: the lower part of the moldings at the top of a building, resting directly on the capitals of the columns

capital: the top part of a column; the three types of capitals are Doric, Ionic, and Corinthian

cornice: the top part of a building's upper moldings, directly above the frieze

entablature: a group of moldings that crown a building; in Greek classical style, it consists of the architrave, frieze, and cornice

facade: the front or face of a building, often having a special design or extra decoration

frieze: a strip of sculptures along the top of a building; the frieze is between the architrave and the cornice

metope: on a frieze, the decorated panel between two triglyphs

pediment: the triangular gable above the entrance to a building

portico: an entryway or porch; a *stoa* is a Greek portico with a row of columns along the front and a wall along the back

triglyph: a vertical divider placed at intervals along a frieze, having three vertical grooves

The amazing theater at Epidaurus is considered one of the high points of all Greek architecture. It could hold 14,000 spectators. Its dimensions and acoustics are perfect. A sound as faint as a piece of paper being torn can be heard from any seat in the theater.

The theater became even more famous after the Romans arrived. During the time of the Roman emperor Hadrian, it was considered the most beautiful theater in the world. It still stands today, one of the best preserved theaters in Greece. Since 1955, an annual festival of classical plays has been held in this place of awesome simplicity.

The Archaeological Site at Delphi

In earliest Greek times, the sanctuary of Delphi, in the shadow of Mt. Parnassus, was consecrated to Mother Earth. Various new settlers arrived around 1200 B.C. In this new culture, men were dominant over women. They wanted the guardian of Delphi to be a god instead of a goddess. Apollo was chosen, and as the years went by, many more monuments were built there to honor Apollo.

From his sanctuary at Delphi, Apollo was believed to deliver oracles—to reveal secrets and future events. At first, he spoke through three women called the Pythias. Later on, there was only one Pythia, who had to be a young virgin. Still later, it was ruled that the Pythia had to be a woman more than fifty years old. The oracle operated once a year, but as requests increased, this was changed to once a month.

The oracle ritual was truly complicated. After petitioners were purified in the Castalian Spring, they sacrificed an animal. Then the Pythia performed a series of rites. Finally she began to speak, answering the petitioners' questions.

The Delphi site includes the temple of Apollo, "treasuries" built by various Greek cities, and a fine theater. The ruins of several temples, one on top of another, have been discovered underneath the temple of Apollo. The city monuments called treasuries are little buildings that look like temples. Pilgrims stored offerings in them.

High up on the hillside is a stadium where the Pythian Games were celebrated. Far below the main sanctuary is a circular *tholos*, the temple of Athena Pronaos. All that remains of it are three columns, with their frieze and cornice.

Under the Guardianship of Apollo
Until 1200 B.C., the sanctuary at Delphi was consecrated to Mother Earth. Later, new peoples brought a culture in which men were dominant over women. They preferred a god as a guardian instead of a goddess, and Apollo was chosen. The site kept growing over the years. Many of its monuments were built in gratitude to Apollo. (*Top photo*) The Agora and Sacred Way of the sanctuary. (*Below, left*) The treasury of the Athenians at Delphi. (*Right*) A bronze sculpture of a charioteer in the museum at Delphi.

The theater and stadium belonged to the temple and were used for religious purposes. The theater can seat 5,000 spectators, who get a beautiful view of the surrounding landscape. On the running track of the stadium, one can still make out two lines marked by tiles. One was the starting line and the other the finish line for races during the Pythian Games.

The Acropolis of Athens

On a rocky, flat-topped hill overlooking Athens is the Acropolis, with a remarkable collection of classical Greek architecture. The Acropolis (Greek for "high city") was built on a plateau 500 feet (150 meters) high, covering an area of about 7.5 acres (3 hectares). Greeks have used the site for more than three thousand years. A fortress there once protected temples and royal palaces. Parts of the original protective wall, known as the Pelasgian Wall, are still standing.

In 480 B.C., the Persians burned all the buildings at the site. But Pericles, the great statesman of Athens, had the Acropolis rebuilt with all the splendor of classical Greece.

One enters the Acropolis through the Propylaea, built in 437 B.C. This is a massive gateway with six Doric columns, grouped in two sets of three columns. On side platforms stand Ionic columns. Just beyond the Propylaea, the tiny Ionic temple of Athena Nike comes into view. It was built by Callicrates in 424 B.C.

The Temple of Temples
Supreme among Greek temples stands the Parthenon. It was built between 447 and 438 B.C. by Ictinus and Callicrates, under the supervision of Phidias. Full of "irregularities" done on purpose, it ends up appearing perfect to the human eye. (*Opposite page, top*) A general view of the Parthenon. (*Below*) The Propylaea, the entrance to the Acropolis.

A Very Special Ionic Temple
The Portico of the Caryatids (*left*) is part of the Erechtheum. The six female figures, more than 6.5 feet (2 meters) tall, function as columns. They are actually copies of the originals. Copies were placed there because the originals would have deteriorated if left in the open air.

Work began in about 421 B.C. on the Erechtheum. This Ionic temple honors Athena and Poseidon, guardians of the city. It stands where the ancient king Erechtheus was buried. One corner of the temple is the famous portico of the caryatids. These are six female figures, each over 6.5 feet (2 meters) high, that function as columns. They were inspired by the *korai*, statues of maidens typical in primitive Greek architecture. The Erechtheum's caryatids are actually copies. The original figures are at the Acropolis Museum, except for one, the best preserved, which is at the British Museum in London.

Between 447 and 438 B.C. the most impressive temple of all, the Parthenon, was built. It was dedicated to Athena Parthenos (Athena the virgin goddess). The architects of this Doric temple were Ictinus and Callicrates, working under the supervision of Phidias. The base of the temple is rectangular, 17 columns long by 8 columns wide. Phidias designed the sculptural decorations that once adorned the Parthenon.

Like other structures at the Acropolis, the Parthenon has had a history of constant change. In A.D. 426, Christian conquerors made the Parthenon a cathedral. Under Turkish rule in the 1400s, it became a mosque. A great disaster took place in 1687. The Turks had their ammunition stored in the Parthenon. As Venetians bombarded Athens, a shell struck the explosives there, causing severe damage. In later centuries, many statues from the temple ended up in Venice.

In the 1800s, most of the decorative sculptures from the Parthenon's frieze and pediments made their way to London. Lord Elgin, the British ambassador to Turkey, persuaded the Turks to let him take them. Now in the British Museum, the sculptures are called the Elgin Marbles.

The majestic Parthenon is a masterpiece of Greek architecture. Why is it considered to be so perfect? Because it is so full of "imperfect" features! Horizontal lines are slightly curved, and vertical lines lean slightly inward. The base on which the columns rest is slightly higher in the middle than at the ends. The columns narrow toward the top, and they are slightly wider in the center than at the base. The columns at the end of a row are wider than those in between.

All these irregular features were done on purpose. The reason? So the Parthenon would appear in perfect proportion to the human eye, whether it was viewed up close or from far away.

These Sites Are Part of the World Heritage

Temple of Apollo the Healer at Bassae. Built in the fifth century B.C., this fine classical temple rises unexpectedly in a rural setting. A number of unusual features, among them the famous Corinthian column, make it unique in the world.

Archaeological Site at Epidaurus. Next to the sanctuary in honor of Asclepius is the famous theater, with a capacity for 14,000 people. Considered one of the greatest works of Greek architecture, it was built in the fourth century B.C.

Archaeological Site at Delphi. Pilgrims from all Greece traveled to Delphi to consult the oracle. They believed that the god Apollo spoke through the mouth of the Pythia. The site includes a number of city monuments, a stadium where the Pythian Games were held, a theater, the temple of Apollo, and the sanctuary of Athena Pronaos.

Acropolis of Athens. Located on a rocky promontory, the Acropolis includes the Propylaea, the temple of Athena Nike, the Erechtheum, and the world-renowned Parthenon. All were built during the Age of Pericles. The Acropolis is considered the definitive work of Greek architecture.

Glossary

acoustics: features of an auditorium that enable sounds to be heard clearly in it

agora: the open marketplace and public square in ancient Greek cities; today, "agoraphobia" is the term for a fear of wide-open spaces

archaeologist: a scientist who learns about the past by studying the remains of ancient objects and buildings

city-state: also called *polis*; a political unit in ancient Greece, made up of a large city and its surrounding land

cothurnus: (plural, cothurni) a thick-soled, laced boot worn by actors in Greek tragedies in order to seem taller

culture: the beliefs, values, skills, and social patterns of a particular group of people

epic poem: a long poem about historical events or about the deeds of a real or legendary hero

hexameter: poetry that has six stressed syllables to a line

lyric poem: a poem expressing personal feelings, often suitable for singing

oracle: a person believed to be speaking for a god in revealing hidden information or future events; a shrine where these revelations take place

oratory: the art of public speaking

philosophy: the search for wisdom; the effort to understand reality

proportion: balance in a design; the relationship of the various parts of a design to each other

pyre: a platform where something is burned

rhapsode: a man who recited poems as a profession in ancient Greece

sanctuary: a place for worship, such as a church or temple; the holy inner part of such a building; a large area, including many buildings, dedicated to religious activity

trilogy: a group of three stories, books, or plays

votive: something offered to seek a favor, fulfill a vow, or give thanks; a votive sanctuary is a holy place where such prayers or offerings are made

Index

Page numbers in boldface type indicate illustrations.

Titles in the World Heritage Series

The Land of the Pharaohs
The Chinese Empire
Ancient Greece
Prehistoric Rock Art
The Roman Empire
Mayan Civilization
Tropical Rain Forests
Inca Civilization
Prehistoric Stone Monuments
Romanesque Art and Architecture
Great Animal Refuges of the World
Coral Reefs

Photo Credits

Cover: F. Lisa Beebe/Incafo; p. 3: L. Ruiz Pastor/Incafo; p. 4: M. Gredler/Incafo; p. 5: L. Ruiz Pastor/Incafo; p. 7: M. Escobar-V. Hemery/Incafo, L. Ruiz Pastor/Incafo; pp. 8-9: L. Ruiz Pastor/Incafo; p. 10: M. Gredler/Incafo; p. 11: L. Ruiz Pastor/Incafo, M. Escobar-V. Hemery/Incafo; pp. 12-13: M. Escobar-V. Hemery/Incafo; p. 15: L. Ruiz Pastor/Incafo; p. 17: L. Ruiz Pastor/Incafo, M. Gredler/Incafo; p. 19: L. Ruiz Pastor/ Incafo; p. 21: L. Ruiz Pastor/Incafo, M. Escobar-V. Hemery/Incafo; p. 23: M. Gredler/ Incafo; p. 25: J. de Vergara/Incafo; p. 27: M. Escobar-V. Hemery/Incafo, M. Gredler/ Incafo; pp. 28 and 29: L. Ruiz Pastor/Incafo; p. 31: L. Ruiz Pastor/Incafo, J. de Vergara/ Incafo, M. Escobar-V. Hemery/Incafo, M. Gredler/Incafo; back cover: P. Sanchez/ Incafo, J. de Vergara/Incafo.

Project Editor, Childrens Press: Ann Heinrichs
Original Text: Marinella Terzi
Subject Consultant: Dr. J. Donald Hughes
Translator: Angela Ruiz
Design: Alberto Caffaratto
Cartography: Modesto Arregui
Drawings: Federico Delicado
Phototypesetting: Publishers Typesetters, Inc.

UNESCO's World Heritage

The United Nations Educational, Scientific, and Cultural Organization (UNESCO) was founded in 1946. Its purpose is to contribute to world peace by promoting cooperation among nations through education, science, and culture. UNESCO believes that such cooperation leads to universal respect for justice, for the rule of law, and for the basic human rights of all people.

UNESCO's many activities include, for example, combatting illiteracy, developing water resources, educating people on the environment, and promoting human rights.

In 1972, UNESCO established its World Heritage Convention. With members from over 100 nations, this international body works to protect cultural and natural wonders throughout the world. These include significant monuments, archaeological sites, geological formations, and natural landscapes. Such treasures, the Convention believes, are part of a World Heritage that belongs to all people. Thus, their preservation is important to us all.

Specialists on the World Heritage Committee have targeted over 300 sites for preservation. Through technical and financial aid, the international community restores, protects, and preserves these sites for future generations.

Volumes in the *World Heritage* series feature spectacular color photographs of various World Heritage sites and explain their historical, cultural, and scientific importance.